CONTENDING FOR THE FAITH,
THE BATTLEGROUND
OF THE MIND

CONTENDING FOR THE FAITH,
THE BATTLEGROUND OF THE MIND

TABITHA HENTON LAMB

ISBN: 978-969-3792-37-9 Print
ISBN: 978-969-3792-36-2 eBook

CONTENTS

Introduction

This book is all about understanding faith in the God of the Bible and His Word as the gateway to power in the spirit. Each one of us has been endowed with a measure of this God-given ability, and we must learn how to regain it for its intended use. Without such an understanding, the church is silently in denial of all the finished work of Jesus Christ on the cross. God is still answering the prayers of the righteous. He is still in the business of working great signs, wonders and miracles, if we would but lay hold of all His promises, which are still yes and amen!

Join me as we journey through the Word of God, allowing Him to reveal the *whole* truth of who He is. We will take this truth and make it the foundation of our new belief system. We will use this truth to tear down and replace all strongholds and high things, all fallacies or false doctrines that have been set by Satan to nullify or water down the word of God in our hearts.

In the first chapter, as presented in a court of law, we will allow the Bible as a living document to become the evidence that He provided to come to a proper resolve that God is who He said He is: the sole Creator of heaven and earth and originator of all life forms. We will then examine how each believer is endued with "The Power to Believe" by showing how God provides evidence in both the seen and unseen realms, and gives "a measure of faith" for each individual to receive His word as truth. In "The Power of Conscience" we examine the role of the conscience as a moral compass guided by the Holy Spirit to help us align our thoughts, motives and actions with God's will.

Against this awareness, we are alerted as to how Satan is still beguiling us just as he did in the garden with Eve. How do some of us fall into the trap of deception? Why do others who know the truth still choose to go their own way? In "Fearless Love" we discuss how fear originates from Satan and how the antidote to fear is God's kind of love – that perfect love that casts out all fear (1 John 4:18).

Then in the topic "Diplomatic Immunity" we look at the divine protection we possess as ambassadors of the Kingdom sealed with the Holy Spirit against all of the onslaughts of Satan. In the final chapter, "Spiritual Combat", we identify the weapons of our warfare to pull down all the strategies of Satan that build strongholds of resistance in our mind to the truth.

In all our study, let us commit to refreshing and replacing all that lies dormant or stagnant in our souls with the Word of Life. Let us regain our God-given strategies to overcome the enemy, particularly when we face hardship in our lives. This is the time to face setbacks without fear but with faith that God has a good purpose in them. This is the time to gird up our mind to contend for the faith that He has delivered to the church, the faith to believe who He is and take Him at His word. This is what we apply to the challenges we face, and this is what we release to the world so that all men will come to know Jesus and put their faith in Him.

Satan, the "god of this world" has blinded the hearts and minds of mankind when they exercise their right of choice not to retain God in their knowledge. But we have the keys to overcome all doubt, and emerge victorious. The kingdom suffers violence and the violent take it by force. Let us contend for our faith! (Matthew 11:12).

Chapter One

FORENSIC EVIDENCE

In a court of law when a person makes a claim, solid evidence is required to show that the person is speaking the truth. Often "forensic evidence" is required, that is, evidence acquired through scientific methods for scrutiny by the court.

God stands, as it were in a court of law to present His case in relation to the many ways He has been misinterpreted by humankind: that He is the Creator and by Him all things exist and hold together. All things that He says in His word can be taken at face value because He provides all the evidence-based knowledge for mankind to completely believe and trust in Him. From His promises to Abraham and Moses in the Old Testament,

He has been faithful in His revelations until now. He does this by what He has chosen to make known concerning who He is and by His deeds and has taken on Himself the responsibility for man to come to know Him, to believe in Him and to love and trust Him.

Although God exists and resides outside of humanity, He has chosen to be intricately and intimately acquainted with us. He began in the Garden of Eden with the promise of a Redeemer. Therefore, He provides the evidence required to show His immutability and sovereignty. In this He is trustworthy, not leaving us without the means to know Him. He gives each of us a measure of faith and the methods to acquire more to know about Him. In this, He is reliable which makes Him consistent; He is faithful and dependable.

In this chapter we are going to look at forensic evidence through the analysis of key data presented "within court proceedings." In a legal context, evidence can be defined as various things presented in court for the purpose of proving or disproving a question under inquiry. It includes testimonies, documents, photographs, maps and video tapes. These are termed as evidence of the case and consist of:

1. The sworn testimony of witnesses, on both direct and cross-examination, regardless of who called the witness.

2. The exhibits which have been received into evidence. These are collected during an inspection through the use of special equipment.

In this study, we are going to use the Bible as our "special equipment" as we exercise our examination of critical evidence by which God has chosen to reveal Himself to us. As reliable documents are produced, we are going to use key scriptures to establish grounds for God and the universe around us. We are going to allow the oldest book since the world began to provide a solid foundation in our search of the truth. In this we should find answers to who God is, the worlds that exist, and the purpose of mankind and all life on earth.

What are we to take into consideration about God and the world around us? He wants us to know that He alone is LORD, that He stretched out the heaven and created them. All things created, seen and unseen, were all created by Him and for Him – the heaven, the earth, the sea and all living things in it – and established by Him. He did not create it without a purpose, for He created it to be inhabited by mankind, animal and plant life. He alone preserves and maintains the life cycles of all living things that were created by Him.

All that was created was made for His glory and this glory He will not divide or share with any other being. Things exist only because He exists and without Him there is no existence of heaven, earth or life on earth. Breath and spirit are His gifts to all human life on earth. There is nothing or no one, including thrones or dominions that are established by men, principalities or powers derived by Satan that can overtake or overthrow Him as all of them exist only because of Him.

> Thus saith the LORD, he that created the heavens, and stretched them out; he that spread forth the earth, and that which cometh out of it; he that giveth breath unto the people upon it, and spirit to them that walk therein (Isaiah 42:5).

> I am the Lord: that is my name: and my glory will I not give to another, neither my praise to graven images (Isaiah 42:8).

> For thus saith the Lord that created the heavens; God himself that formed the earth and made it; he hath established it, he created it not in vain, he

formed it to be inhabited: I am the Lord and there is none else (Isaiah 45:18).

And he is before all things and by Him all things consist (Colossians 1:17).

Through faith we understand that the worlds were framed by the word of God so that things which are seen were not made of things which do appear (Hebrews 11:3).

All things were made by him; and without him was not anything made that was made (John 1:3).

For by him were all things created, that are in heaven, and that are on the earth, visible and invisible, whether they be thrones, or dominions or principalities, or powers: all things were created by him and for him (Colossians 1:16).

Thou, even thou, art LORD alone; thou hast made heaven, the heaven of heavens, with all their host, the earth, and all things that are threin, the seas, and all that is therein, and thou pre-servest them all; and the host of heaven worshippeth thee (Nehemiah 9:6).

Satan, on the other hand, is finite in all of his abilities, schemes and power. If he were not, he would be the equal to God – and we know this is not true. The word of God reveals through the prophet Ezekiel that Satan is only a created being: "Thou wast perfect in thy ways from the day that thou wast **created**, till iniquity was found in thee" (Ezekiel 28:15).

God wants things to go well for all humanity on earth. In His desire for our good, He provides the means or the ability for man to achieve such wellness. If man can have a heart in him to fear Him, it will propel him to keep His commandments and to have a reverential fear of Him. Such a heart will cause man to pay heed to his thoughts, words and his actions to take care to please Him with no desire or inclination apart from Him.

> O that there were such an heart in them, that they would fear me, and keep all my commandments always, that it might be well with them, and with their children for ever! (Deuteronomy 5:29)

A proper concept of who God is, as He has revealed in His word and promises to us, is therefore necessary. He is trustworthy and omnipotent in any situation we face in life. He is approachable, kind and gentle and has a compassionate nature. He is omniscient and He will not change. With this foundation, we can understand what He has given to man for him to believe.

If therefore we can put Satan in proper perspective in our hearts and mind, we can establish the kind of faith that was once delivered to the church. This is the greatest battle in the life of a believer. If we win here, we overcome. God has no equal or no rival. Who can contend with Him? This is where we put Satan in his place concerning who he is in comparison to God.

We can learn much of the nature of God from Job's account as well as the boundaries set that limited how far Satan could touch God's righteous servant.

JOB QUESTIONS GOD

Here was a man who was blameless and upright, who feared God and shunned evil. Job found himself in a showdown between God and Satan and called God to account for all the calamities that were afflicting him.

Unknown to Job, there had been a dialogue between Satan and God. Satan wanted to prove that Job served God only because things were going well for him and not because he loved Him. He believed Job would have behaved differently if things did not go so favorably towards Him.

> "Does Job fear God for nothing? Have You not made a hedge around him, around his household, and around all that he has on every side? You have blessed the work of his hands, and his possessions have increased in the land. But now, stretch out Your hand and touch all that he has, and he will surely curse You to Your face!"

> And the LORD said to Satan, "Behold, all that he has *is* in your power; **only do not lay a hand on his *person*"** (Job 1:9-11 NKJV).

So as a test of Job's loyalty, Satan was given permission to afflict Job though not to take his life. Satan then literally caused one of the worst trials that ever happened to mankind to happen to Job in two waves of calamity, first his children and possessions and then his own health. Even so, God was still in control and limited the power of Satan.

Satan moved against Job to such a degree that Job accused God, "What have I done?" He requested an audience that he might plead his own case calling God to account for the crisis he faced. He thought the evil against him was at the hand of God. But it was Satan at work testing four aspects of his wellbeing:

- his children – fruitfulness

- his possessions – prosperity

- his body – sickness

- his soul – from peace and tranquility to grief and anguish

Job's suffering was so great that he could not properly identify who the real enemy was, opening himself into believing the lying accusations of Satan against God. In the anguish and confusion of his soul, aggravated by the unwarranted attacks on his own integrity by his friends and even his wife, Job made many untrue statements about God. But behind it all was Satan who added to all the afflictions the terrorizing of Job's soul to move it into believing God was against him.

In his limited capacity and tormented by all his suffering, Job did not understand that the glory of God was tied to all this testing. We too, when we are tested, even though we cannot understand what is happening, must come to a resolve that only the glory of God is what ultimately matters. This is what will give us steely determination to embrace our condition, saying as Jesus did, "Nevertheless not as I will for things to go My way, but as You will." This takes enormous faith and trust in God. Nevertheless, let us do as Jesus did when He said,

"Father, for this reason came I into the world to die for it. I may not like this; however, it is My purpose to secure Your glory." (John 12:27-28)

Job took no comfort in his friends who accused him of sinning, and he retaliated by calling them "quacks" and "miserable comforters." Job is so disappointed in human comfort, he even calls the animal life to the stand to witness for him: "But ask now the beasts, and they shall teach thee; and the fowls of the air, and they shall tell thee: Or speak to the earth, and it shall teach you; let the fish of the sea inform you who knoweth not in all these that the hand of the LORD hath wrought this? In whose hand is the soul of every living thing, and the breath of all mankind" (Job 12:7-8).

In his distorted notion of God through such suffering, Job made seventy-four false statements concerning God, which we know were initiated by Satan. Just as the serpent did to Eve's mind, Satan moved him to accuse God of deeds which were not orchestrated by Him. We see his state of disillusion and sense of betrayal by God in such statements as:

The Lord taketh away (Job 1:21).

Shall we not receive evil? (2:10)

… the terrors of God do set themselves in array against me (6:4).

God scares me with dreams and terrifies me through visions (7:14).

He breaks me with tempest (9:17).

One dieth in his full strength, being wholly at ease and quiet. And another dieth in the bitterness of his soul, and never eateth with pleasure (21:23, 25).

He destroys the perfect with the wicked (9:22).

He will laugh at the trial of the innocent (9:23).

He has given the earth to the wicked (9:28).

You know I am not wicked, yet You destroy me (10:7-8).

You hunt me as a fierce lion (10:16).

God has overthrown me (19:6).

There is no injustice from Him (19:7).

… kindled his wrath against me (19:11).

The Almighty troubles me (23:16).

You are become cruel to me (30:21).

God has taken away my judgement (27:2).

But God is fair and honors the petition of Job to enter into His courtroom. He answers Job's statements in two phases just as Job was tested in two phases.

First, God provides Job with forensic evidence against his accusations against Him (Job 38 and 39). Here He deals with Job's accusations from a cosmic perspective. He presents before the witness stand His secret workings of the universe concerning creation and the many facets of nature, including the abundant care and well-being of all His animal creatures.

Secondly, He deals with Job's accusations based on his finite worldview. This caused him to make inaccurate statements about God due to his limited capacity to fathom the vast wisdom and counsel of God and His compassionate character. In his efforts, he tried to reduce God to human logic, human terms and reasoning.

These selected verses from Job chapter 38 will give a picture of His arguments:

[1]Then the LORD answered Job out of the whirlwind, and said, [2]Who is this that darkeneth counsel by words without knowledge? [3]Gird up now thy loins like a man; for I will demand of thee, and answer thou me. [4]Where wast thou when I laid the foundations of the earth? declare, if thou hast understanding. [5]Who hath laid the measures thereof, if thou knowest? or who hath stretched the line

upon it? [6] Whereupon are the foundations thereof fastened? or who laid the corner stone thereof;

[7] When the morning stars sang together, and all the sons of God shouted for joy?

[12] Hast thou commanded the morning since thy days; and caused the dayspring to know his place; [13] That it might take hold of the ends of the earth, that the wicked might be shaken out of it?

[19] Where is the way where light dwelleth? and as for darkness, where is the place thereof,

[33] Knowest thou the ordinances of heaven? canst thou set the dominion thereof in the earth? [34] Canst thou lift up thy voice to the clouds, that abundance of waters may cover thee

[35] Canst thou send lightnings, that they may go and say unto thee, Here

we are? [36] Who hath put wisdom in the inward parts? or who hath given understanding to the heart?

God then challenged Job in this manner, "Can you sit over the earth as Creator of the cosmos and the earth? Answer these questions. Are you equipped with the kind of wisdom to know the depth of the earth or the animals in it? Are you fit to care and provide for them? If you cannot how can you disannul my judgment or my counsel simply because you cannot comprehend Me in your finite mind?"

Here are some of the words God used to challenge His accuser in Job 40:

> [2] Shall he that contendeth with the Almighty instruct him? He that reproveth God, let him answer it ... [7] Gird up thy loins now like a man: I will demand of thee, and declare thou unto me. [8] Wilt thou also disannul my

judgment? wilt thou condemn me, that thou mayest be righteous? ⁹ Hast thou an arm like God? or canst thou thunder with a voice like him? ¹⁰ Deck thyself now with majesty and excellency; and array thyself with glory and beauty … ¹⁴ Then will I also confess unto thee that thine own right hand can save thee.

In the face of such overwhelming evidence of the beneficence and might of His Creator, what could Job say? All he could do was bow down to God meekly and repent.

"I know that You can do everything, And that no purpose *of Yours* can be withheld from You … Therefore I have uttered what I did not understand, Things too wonderful for me, which I did not know … I have heard of You by the hearing of the ear, But now my eye sees You. Therefore I abhor *myself,* and repent in dust and ashes" (Job 42:2, 3, 5-6).

God was very gracious to His servant. He understood his anguish over both his personal suffering and the provocation by his friends with their limited understanding of Job's integrity and the immensity of who God was. God had been gracious enough to honor his servant's request and allow him to present his case in His courtroom. He honored Job also in his words not because they were true – for this Job was rebuked and corrected – but because they truly came out of the heart of a hurting man whose prayer, tears and supplications had come before his Maker.

Chapter Two

THE POWER TO BELIEVE

God's promises are radical, and will require faith to stand on. But He supplies us with the faith to make a demand on His promises and hold on to them until they manifest. Although belief is required, true faith goes beyond belief. Faith (Greek *pistis*) is the divine ability needed to believe what God reveals to us. It is God's warranty to solidify that what He reveals will come to pass (I John 5:4). Faith cannot be drummed up by human effort. Only God can give faith, and He has given each of us a certain measure of faith (Romans 12:3) as He sees fit.

Hebrews 11:1 in the Amplified version says:

> Now faith is the assurance (title deed, confirmation) of things hoped for (divinely guaranteed), and the evidence of things not seen [the conviction of their reality—faith comprehends as fact what cannot be experienced by the physical senses].

Faith comes with the **assurance** (Greek *hupostasis*) or support, groundwork, and evidence, which gives a kind of certainty and confidence to substantiate what we hope for. Faith opens our spiritual eyes to see what is not visible and to believe. Faith is man's response to what God has revealed simply by trusting in His character and His word. By faith, we come to believe that the worlds were framed by the word of God. Faith causes us to know that the will of God for us is good. Abraham laid hold of the will of God for his life. It was the promise given him by God by grace and he refused to let it go.

Faith enables us to receive the gospel message. What is the gospel? It is the power of God to salvation for all who choose to believe in Jesus Christ. The gospel is the outcome of His goodness and good will toward man. If we can believe His promises throughout the Old Testament, we can believe and testify of all He has made available through His Son: for provision, for healing, restoration, salvation of loved ones and all those who are lost in sin. If this gospel is good news, then nothing else will condemn the soul of men more than doubt. "He that believeth and is baptized shall be saved; but **he that believeth not shall be damned**" (Mark 16:16).

And when we are made right with God, or justified, faith has completed its perfect work. To complete the process of justification, we must first believe in Jesus as our Savior (Galatians 2:16).

For therein is the **righteousness** of God **revealed** from faith to faith **as it**

is written the just shall live by faith (Romans 1:16-17).

This means that those who are just in God's eyes become so by their faith in Him. By contrast, the **wrath of God** is revealed **against** all ungodliness and unrighteousness of men, who hold the truth but chose not to live by it. God's righteousness as revealed in the gospel and founded upon faith is the only method approved by Him for salvation to all who will believe in Him.

Therefore, we must live a disciplined life of continued faith daily – to wake up in faith, to walk out each day in faith and to end the day in faith. This is our walk each day while there is breath and life in us. I must wake up in faith and remain there to offer the day to God as a testimony of one who stands honorable in faith towards Him.

However, there is a consequence to those who remain in ungodliness and unrighteousness alike. The wrath of God comes upon all those who possess the truth but continue to live and function as if they do not have the power to believe. "For the wrath of God is revealed from heaven against all ungodliness and unrighteousness of men, who hold the truth in unrighteousness" (Romans 1:18). Is this not like Eve, holding the truth but denying it?

God has chosen to reveal all that is required for one to put on belief in Him. But, in the case of those who continue in ungodliness and unrighteousness, this shows their lack of belief in Him. He has already proven His existence by the revealing of nature's attributes from the creation of the world which are clearly seen and demonstrate His eternal power and Godhead. In light of such truth we are without excuse if we still do not believe (Romans 1:18).

> Because that which may be known of God is manifest in them: for God hath shewed it unto them. For the **invisible things** of him from the creation

of the world are clearly seen being **understood** by the things which are made, and even his eternal power and Godhead; so that they are **without excuse** (Romans 1:19-20).

What is this reason for their error?

Because that, **when they knew God, they glorified him not** as God. Neither **were thankful: but became** vain in their imaginations, and their foolish heart was **darkened. Professing** themselves to be wise, they **became fools.** And **changed** the glory of the uncorruptible God into an image made like corruptible man, and to birds, and four footed beast, and creeping things (Romans 1:21-23).

We may consider ourselves exempt from such apostasy because we have not made any visible idols before Him. However, we must search our hearts to find the gods we have fashioned within: these are the idols of the heart. Although we know Him, we fail to glorify and honor Him according to the truth we have come to know of Him. Instead we become unthankful, which leads us into becoming vain in what we imagine. Without the light of God, our hearts have become foolish and darkened; the light of God is unable to penetrate our hearts to reveal the true content of what is hidden there, so we are left to our own devices.

Here is the result of such a state. God responds to this kind of life choice. He gives them over to uncleanness through the lust of their own hearts. Their foolish hearts, which have become darkened, are now turned over to dishonor their own bodies between themselves. How will this be displayed? Here are the signs: the souls of men and women are defiled and given over to lust for their own gender, men with men and woman with woman. Why? Because they **worshiped created things** rather than God. Because **they changed the truth** of God for a lie and **worshiped and served** the creature more than the Creator, who is blessed forever. Amen. Their worship of creation and not the Creator brought about idol worship and led to sexual perversion.

Why did God give such people over to this kind of sin? "And even as **they did not like to retain God in their knowledge**, God gave them over to a reprobate mind, to do those things which are not convenient" (Romans 1:28 – NASB translates "not convenient" to "not proper").

What are the specific acts that are "not proper"?

> For this cause **God gave them up** unto
> vile **affections**: for **even the women**
> did change the **natural use** into that
> which is against nature: And likewise
> **also the man** leaving the **natural use**
> of the women, burned in their lust
> one toward another: **men with men**
> working that which is unseemly, and

receiving in themselves that recompense of the error which was met (Romans 1:24-25).

Homosexuality is a subject we feel uncomfortable talking about but we must deal with it. If we have wondered why the rise of such appetites, this is the key. These perversions are not from God, nor are they pleasing to Him. They are not approved of Him. We can see here clearly they are a result of the heart that is turned away from Him, given over to uncleanness because of the lust of the heart.

What are the characteristics of ungodliness and the fruits of unrighteousness?

> … **unrighteousness, fornication, wickedness, covetousness, maliciousness, full of envy, murder, debate, deceit, malignity, whisperers, backbiters, haters of God, despiteful, proud, boasters, inventors of evil things, disobedient to parents:**

Without understanding, covenant breakers, without natural affections, implacable, unmerciful: Who knowing the judgment of God, that they which commit such things are worthy of death, not only do the same, but have pleasure in them that do them (Romans 1:29-32).

Tribulation and anguish is upon every soul that does evil, for God is no respecter of persons.

On the other hand, if we obey God's commands and continue to do good, we will pursue those things that are from above. Even though we live in the flesh, we now live a new life through faith in Jesus. We are dead to the sin nature and alive by faith through Christ. We are alive to the life in the body but dead to the works of sin owing nothing to it. Our body now belongs to Christ to live for God. We must not allow ourselves to be drawn away from the faith in the gospel to put our faith in our human efforts. We must come to know the truth, to believe and continue in the truth that we know and to be doers of the truth we apprehend (Galatians 3:1). We must worship God and serve Him with the whole heart and give ourselves completely to Him in word, in deed and in truth.

We must be careful of not being carried away by other doctrines or becoming a law unto ourselves lest we become perverters of the true gospel of Christ (Galatians 3:1-4). Do not add or omit anything in the word to alter the truth of the foundation of the gospel that was already laid. Eve added to the word of God by including "neither shall ye touch it" when the serpent asked whether God had commanded them not to eat all the fruit in the garden (Hebrews 6:1). When the serpent prompted her to touch the fruit, nothing happened because there was no such command. This emboldened her to think, "Oh, nothing happened when I touched it, so maybe the serpent is right; nothing will happen if I eat it." The serpent capitalized on this error.

So in that moment, Satan used the opportunity to nullify the word of God in her heart.

Abraham was justified because he laid hold of the promise of God and refused to let it go. By his relentless faith, he came to a position of believing without a shadow of a doubt that he belonged to God. That knowledge was his security. "… the word of the LORD came to Abram in a vision, saying, "Do not be afraid, Abram. **I *am* your shield, your exceedingly great reward"** (Genesis 15:1). We too must lay hold of this same relentless faith in the gospel and refuse to let it go as if it is our last resort or only hope, because in reality it is (Galatians 3:11).

We remain the just by continuing to live by faith in our daily lives (Romans 1:17). We must hold on to obedience to the word of God at all costs, and never forsake it. If we believe we are saved; if not we are condemned (Deuteronomy 28:15).

Believing in the word of God entails giving up our right to live the way we choose and become followers of Christ. This will require us to walk away from the lures and desires of the world with no palate for the delights laid out before us. This is how we become true children of God. Just as Abraham was told by God to get himself away from his kindred, and to abandon their way of life, traditions and culture, it is no different for us. This may not require a physical relocation but it will require walking away from the world's way of doing life. This includes all of its traditions or false belief systems, which are sure to provoke a falling away from Christ (Mark 16:16).

Death was once our only fate because of sin but God has given an opportunity for each person to choose life for himself. Each of us has the opportunity to reap the harvest of our own sowing, no longer that of Adam. How is this possible? By choosing Christ. This will require us to forsake all the pursuits of our past life and embrace the new: we must give ourselves up completely over to it. However, we must first believe in Jesus and not in confession alone, but by reflecting it in the way we choose to live our lives. We must walk away completely from the kingdom of darkness with no part of it remaining. We must deny and crucify the flesh by continuous obedience to His way in every situation we face.

For those who truly seek union with Christ, this is the only way. This empowers us to walk away from a life of sin, and be saved from the destruction that comes as its reward. I cannot emphasize enough that the most important requirement is BELIEF in Jesus. This is the foundation of the Christian faith. In this, it is imperative that we examine the system founded by our belief, search it out and find out what we believe to be more powerful than Jesus. Is it the doctor's report; is it rejection, poverty, demonic intrusion? Is it fear? Whatever this false belief system, we must uproot it to its total annihilation. We do this by going to the word of God and finding the true answer to the situation at hand. Nothing can impede you from finding the specific promise of God for your situation. He has the perfect solution for every situation. This is where your warfare begins. You must drive out everything in the belief system that is contrary to the truth.

GOD'S KINGDOM NOT OF THIS WORLD

When Pontius Pilate asked Jesus at His trial what the truth was, Jesus said He had come into the world to bear witness to the truth. "To this end was I born, and for this cause came I into the world, that I should bear witness unto the truth. Every one that is of the truth heareth my voice" (John 18:37). Though He was in this world, He was not of it and neither did He depend on its systems, its strategies or methods. This is the perfect model of how we are to operate in this world's system.

Jesus knew this was a spiritual battle between Himself and Satan; therefore He would not allow His disciples to use human methods to defend

Him. He rebuked Peter for using his sword to cut off the ear of the high priest's servant. And even though the zealots wanted to make Him an earthly king, He knew He was the King of another realm, acknowledging that the "ruler of this world" was Satan (John 14:30). He was in a spiritual battle with spiritual enemies for spiritual purposes. Although He saw earthly opposition, He did not allow it to affect His resolve to complete His mission.

He did not misuse His power by bending to the human inclination to defend oneself. How close this mirrors the temptation in the wilderness when Satan tempted Him to cast Himself down from a high place to demonstrate how God's angels would bear him up, misusing Psalm 91:11-12! He maintained the same discipline during the conversation with Pontius Pilate.

When Jesus was delivered to Pilate, Pilate asked, "Art thou the King of the Jews?"

Jesus answered, "My kingdom is not of this world: if my kingdom were of this world, then would my servants fight, that I should not be delivered to the Jews: but now is my kingdom not from hence."

Here was the reason He came into the world: to be a witness to the Kingdom for which He was set as King. He had come into the world to break the power of sin and of death and to destroy the works of the devil and render him powerless against mankind. He was to be brought into public that men could see him and bring him to open shame. But, in the end, at His resurrection, having spoiled principalities and powers, it was them that He made an open show of, triumphing over them in it (Colossians 2:15).

Now was His turn to put His enemy and ours on display and bring them to shame. Just as Satan was exposed in the garden as the true enemy of God and man, Jesus came to expose this enemy at

His resurrection: to show him up for who he is and to bring him to ruin. For the weapons of our warfare are not carnal but spiritual, and God would not have us ignorant of Satan's devices. He has taken great care and caution to reveal this enemy to us along with the weapons he will use against us. With this knowledge and understanding, we are also properly equipped for battle as long as we use the right weapons He has both instituted and given to us.

The primary source of our power is the word of God. We have to eat it daily as Jesus teaches us: man shall not live by bread alone but by every word that proceeds out of the mouth of God. Therefore do not seek just to feed, fuel and nourish the physical man only but seek also to feed, fuel and nourish the spiritual man. This is the foundation of belief and faith.

God gave Adam and Eve the power to believe. Together with that power to believe, they had their own will and freedom to exercise their choice. In spite of that power and freedom, they chose to go their own way, contrary to God and His word.

In the next chapter we will learn about the three failures that made Adam and Eve's tenure in paradise a short lived one. We will discover how to identify the three failures in our own lives, and understand how each one prohibits humanity from obeying God and His word.

Chapter Three

THE THREE FAILURES

The three failures of humanity are: Doubt, Fear and Unbelief. These all have one aim: to produce a failure to believe with the primary intent of reaching unbelief. Whether it is due to insufficient evidence or fear or ignorance, to not believe is to deny the power and the word of God's ability to produce faith. Unbelief has great eternal consequences, for all liars and doubters will have their part in the lake of fire. I pray we can see the necessity of receiving the gift of faith from God without doubting.

"But without faith it is impossible to please him: for he that cometh to God must believe that he is, and that he is a rewarder of them that diligently seek him" (Hebrews 11:6). Without faith it is absolutely impossible to please the Lord. Everything begins and ends in faith. We must first believe, then continue in faith or else nothing we do will please God.

> But let him ask in faith, nothing wavering. For he that wavereth is like a wave of the sea driven with the wind and tossed. For let not that man think that he shall receive any thing of the Lord. A double minded man is unstable in all his ways (James 1:6-8).

Doubt, on the other hand, is a lack of confidence: distrust, an inclination not to believe or accept; it embodies uncertainty or a belief or opinion that often interferes with decision-making, a deliberate suspension of judgment: "**For all of this, they sinned still** and **believed** not for his wondrous works. Therefore their days did **he consume** in vanity and their years in trouble" (Psalm 78:32-33). Does it mean that, because of doubt, all we need is more faith to acquire the benefits promised?

No, doubt is much more insidious. Its end is to **disbelieve** and **constantly deny the truth** – using every excuse to not believe what is true. Through holding on to doubt, we are in danger of being beguiled, misled, deluded, led astray and eventually deceived. Deceived implies believing in a false idea or belief system.

Doubt is cunning because it hides behind a veil. This is the devil's greatest weapon against humanity because it all seems so innocent. But let us go back to its beginnings to see how it evolves.

The serpent caused the unsuspecting Eve not to believe what God said through the power of thought manipulation. He manipulated her mind from a position of knowing the truth to a state of unbelief. He caused her thought process to operate as if it did not believe. To understand the weapon of doubt, we must define the strategy for its purpose or use. In Eve's case, the devil caused her to

question the truth, which led her to waver in what she knew to be true.

What are the practices of doubt? Doubt establishes strongholds in the mind to restrict and prohibit us from taking God at His word. This is where the foundation must be destroyed and uprooted. We must ask ourselves: what kind of doubts lurk in our subconscious that strengthen disobedience and resistance to His word? What is it that is robbing us of our faith or our ability to believe? What subtle lie has the enemy presented that we have received and accepted ownership of? What is that something that has just enough truth to make it plausible?

Unbelief is a byproduct of the carnal mind, which is founded on sense knowledge. What are you trying to believe that requires more faith and less sense knowledge? The senses work collectively with the appetites making the soul the battleground. The senses are what feed strongholds in our lives. They war continuously against faith and the Spirit.

On the other hand, faith is what the spirit uses to dominate the five senses so that we walk by faith and not by sight. With faith, we speak out those things that are not as though they were. Faith allows us to have the same mind that is in Christ Jesus. It causes us to go to God and petition Him for what we desire with confidence. It causes us to incline our ear to the Good Shepherd's voice and to blot out the other voices assailing us. Through faith, we listen only to words that promise obedience to God and His word. Faith enables us to use our mouth and eyes for what they are designed for – to taste and see that the Lord is good and to desire to feast on His word.

Faith is a powerhouse tool against the five senses and unbelief. If you shut down the five senses, you can eliminate doubt and pull down strongholds and all things contrary to the truth of who God is. Matthew 17:20 says, "If ye have faith as a grain of mustard seed, ye shall say unto this mountain, Remove hence to yonder place; and it shall remove; and nothing shall be impossible unto you."

What strongholds in our mind hinder us from receiving all that we need from God? Can you identify and define them? Mark 16:17 talks of the signs that accompany the one who believes: "And these signs shall follow them that believe. In My name, they shall cast out devils; they shall speak with new tongues, and they shall take up serpents, and if they drink any deadly thing, it shall not hurt them; they shall lay hands on the sick and they shall recover." Are we denying any of these signs in our confrontation with evil because of unbelief, ignorance or misinterpreting the word? Perhaps, we have been taught that signs, wonders and miracles –even speaking in tongues – were signs given to the early church but do not apply to the modern church. If we hold such beliefs, then we have a stronghold of unbelief possessing "a form of godliness, but denying the power thereof" (2 Timothy 3:5).

Perhaps we do not step out in faith to do as the word says because a stronghold of fear has formed in us. So we are fearful of what people say. "Fearful" comes from the Greek word *deilos*, which means "cowardly." "To be fearful" is "to be apprehensive" or "to be afraid to be disturbed by fear." Fearfulness often implies a timorous or worrying temperament or a kind of phobia. What is blocking your faith from arising? Is it a phobia? Could it be the fear of man?

The first time we see fear make its appearance was in Adam and Eve. Adam and Eve were in hiding having eaten the fruit because they saw their own nakedness and were ashamed. When God asked Adam why he was hiding, it's interesting to see how Adam replied: "I heard thy voice and was afraid because I was naked" (Genesis 3:10).

Let's see how the scene played out in Genesis 3.

And the eyes of them both were opened, and they knew they were naked: and they **sewed fig leaves** together, and made **themselves** aprons. And they heard the voice of the LORD God walking in the garden in the cool of the day: and Adam and his wife hid themselves from the presence of the LORD God among the trees of the garden.

And the LORD God called unto Adam, and said unto him, where art thou?

And he said, I heard thy voice in the garden and I was afraid, because I was naked: and I hid myself.

Fear had made its entrance immediately in the soul of mankind after they heard the voice of God in the garden. There was no fear prior to this, neither was there an occasion for it.

What does fear cause us to do and why? Fear causes us to be aware of our nakedness, our lack, our shortcomings, our sin and guilt. We fear because we are ashamed of ourselves and are afraid of being exposed and judged by others. But we have already judged ourselves.

We can see what caused fear from the beginning and we can also see the reward for fear in the last book of the bible. "But the **fearful and unbelieving** are guaranteed a reward as their inheritance, their part in the lake of fire and brimstone: which is the second death" (Revelation 21:8). Notice here how fear is closely associated with unbelief because fear shuts our eyes to faith in God's abundant mercy and the miracle-working power of the Almighty.

Fear is one of the prime strategies of Satan. The time had come for him to exercise the next phase of his plan, the play-out of a mastermind to dominate the soul of all mankind. In this we can see the stages of his pre-determined plan against God and humanity unfold in the move of civil society to establish its own governance without God, the Bible, the knowledge of the saving power of Jesus Christ.

Doubt, unbelief and disobedience, which closed the door to faith, gave access to fear in the soul of man. What is unbelief? The failure to take God at every one of His words. Unbelief implies incredulity or skepticism especially in matters of faith in God. The Greek word *apistos* describes an unbeliever or one without faith.

Satan's strategy caused Eve to "unbelieve" or to abandon what she knew to be true. She gave herself over to doubt, both in God's word and His integrity. This is what caused disobedience. It is doubt that damns the souls. How many times have we as Christians been defeated by this same tactic. The first thought may look spontaneous as if it was initiated by ourselves; but Satan always has an end goal in mind. Unknown to her, he had an end goal for her, just as he does for all of humanity. His motive is to manipulate the word of truth until we allow our thoughts to become muddied as if we never knew the truth.

So we alter the word so that it loses its cutting edge and becomes weak: "To him that knoweth to do good and doeth it not to him it is sin" (James 4:17). We must be careful of changing the word of God to make it excusable for us to operate as if we did not know the truth. This is inexcusable to God and it is not without consequence.

This would never have happened if Adam and Eve had a reverential fear of God. This meant an awareness of His presence, an awe of Him, a respect for and submission to His words, and therefore obedience to Him in all aspects of life. A reverential fear of God is the right concept of Him and will guard our hearts. This is what will cause us to walk upright before Him. Psalms 111:10 tells us how this fear is equated with wisdom, "The fear of the LORD is the beginning of wisdom; A good understanding have all those who do His commandments …" and Psalm 19:9 says that "The fear of the LORD is clean, enduring forever; The judgments of the LORD are true; they are righteous altogether."

Adam and Eve were once comfortable in the presence of their Father and would meet with Him in the cool of the day. Had they become too familiar with Him and thus began to lose that reverential fear? Now they were fearful of meeting Him. They heard the voice of the LORD walking in the garden and this brought fear, tremor and dread to the degree they hid themselves from Him. The thought of facing God brought terror in meeting the consequences of their action.

Adam the head of this household now had to face the God who gave him provision, substance, a help meet for companionship, and a strategic plan for humanity. This was the one who gave precise instructions concerning the boundaries to maintain for their own safety and to protect the garden from intruders; it was a command given for protection and not for control. Adam was also warned of the repercussion if they made the decision to eat: death. He did not hold this truth of God in his heart even when he knew the penalty would be death. He did not fear death enough not to eat of the fruit. Now death is man's greatest fear.

In this Satan has also deceived. He has so twisted the instruction of God that man now fears physical death above spiritual death. Can you imagine this now playing over and over in our minds, that mankind would experience death? Can you imagine the thoughts that plagued the mind once fear set in? Not knowing the consequence had already befallen them they lived in continuous terror of dying the physical death when the most crucial death had already taken place. The most powerful blow had already been served. Death was served to the spiritual life of all of humanity.

Jesus said that Satan was a murderer from the beginning. When he speaks a lie he speaks of his own words and not those from God.

> **Ye are of your father the devil**, and the lust of your father ye will do. **He was a murderer** from the beginning, and **abode not** in the truth, because there is **no truth in him**. When he speaketh a lie, he speaketh of his own: for **he is a liar**, and the father of it (John 8:44).

Satan has now established himself as the ruler of this world, which even Jesus admitted (John 14:30; John 16:11) and the apostle Paul called him "the god of this world": "… the god of this world hath blinded the minds of them which believe not, lest the light of the glorious gospel of Christ, who is the image of God, should shine unto them" (2 Corinthians 4:4). Therefore mankind is prone to his lies and is impervious to the gospel message.

Jesus said, "And because I tell you the truth, ye believe me not. And if I say the truth, why do you believe me not? He that is of God heareth God's words: ye hear them not, **because** ye are not of God (John 8:45-47).

If we truly believed in God's words, we would never have to fear death. For Jesus said, "verily, I say unto you, If a man keep my saying, he shall never see death (John 8:51). He will never experience what he fears most. But this is exactly what Jesus paid the price for. He stripped Satan of the right of use against humanity, and defeated him at the cross. Jesus is the resurrection and the life, "I am the resurrection, and the life: he that believeth in me, though he were dead, yet shall he live" (John 11:25). With that the power of sin and death has also been defeated. Death no longer has its sting against humanity unless they knowingly forfeit this promise and provision from God.

Adam and Eve had exchanged their first security in God for self-consciousness. This self-consciousness, which once fueled their pride and independence, would now come back to cause torment and fear, constantly reminding them of the consequences of their deed. They did not realize what they had until they lost it. On the other hand, we have no concept of what they experienced prior to their deed. It is hard for the human mind to fathom this kind of relationship with God, the true security a child has in a parent. This reality is difficult because of the guilt-stained conscience of man outside of Christ. We have both awareness of our sin and errors and we are tormented by it with no means of relief.

In the next chapter we are going to look into the power of the conscience. What is conscience and its intended role? How does it mitigate our tendency to sin? When does it abuse this role and allow itself to be set to operate against us?

THE POWER OF CONSCIENCE

If Adam and Eve had first listened to their inner voice when tempted, they would not have acted in such haste. They would have taken a step back to access the promises of Satan against the specific command of God.

What is this inner voice? It is our conscience. Conscience is a person's moral compass of right and wrong, which acts as a guide to one's behavior. It carries the consciousness of the moral goodness or blameworthiness of one's own conduct, intentions, or character together with the sense of obligation to do the right thing. The Cambridge dictionary explains it more simply as "the part of you that judges how moral your own actions are and makes you feel guilty about bad things that you have done or things you feel responsible for." As part of our moral faculty, our conscience acts as a check to behavior arising from our immediate impulses or emotions which are sense-based. Such a moral faculty has been given by God to us all.

According to the Matthew Henry Commentary, our heart has its own self-reflecting power to judge our actions, a God-given noble ability to evaluate our own spirits, our dispositions, and actions, and pass a judgment upon our state towards God. The moral conscience can act as a witness, judge or executioner. It either accuses or it excuses, condemns or justifies. It warns us if we are taking a wrong step and it helps us correct error.

Now, while conscience is always based on an individual's sense of right and wrong due to their socialization, as Christians, our ethics and morals are governed by the word of God. This is the standard set by God to judge our thoughts as well as the outcome of our deeds. The Spirit of man is the candle of the Lord, whose duty is to search the inward part of man to scrutinize and to bring to view the private and secret accounts of the inner man. It examines not only our outward behavior but also our inward motives.

> For the word of God *is* living and powerful, and sharper than any two-edged sword, piercing even to the division of soul and spirit, and of joints and marrow, and is a **discerner of the thoughts and intents of the heart** (Hebrews 4:12 NKJV).

David cried out to God, "Examine me, O LORD, and prove me; Try my reins and my heart" in Psalm 26:2 at a time when he was persecuted by his enemies, and appealed to God for vindication. He had a conscience but he by-passed it when he committed adultery with Bathsheba and remained in that sin for a whole year until he was confronted by the prophet Nathan (2 Samuel 12).

Like David, Adam and Eve's conscience by-passed them initially, but after their sin, a guilty conscience opened their eyes to their nakedness and shame. It caused them to hide from themselves and ultimately from God. No longer were they able to walk with Him because the condemnation was so heavy. Is this not a true reflection of us all when we fall short of obedience to Him?

However, we should not be bound by our human conscience as it is not the ultimate judge. Even though there may be an inner witness in our conscience, God has authority over it through the Holy Spirit He gives us. God searches and evaluates the heart according to His righteous judgment and He purifies it to bring about godly morality and ethics in every situation. So when we make ourselves the sole judge of our behavior we set ourselves up for condemnation. We become so conscious of our sin and offense against God's absolute standards that we arbitrarily find ourselves guilty, unfit for use, and doomed to punishment or loss of rights. This may or may not be the true picture and we need to inquire of the Lord, just as David did.

However, whether we feel condemned or not, there is always an escape route as the Apostle Paul reveals in Romans 8. This escape route is for all those who are in Christ, and who do not pursue the things of the flesh. And so we have to ask ourselves whom we are giving our deeds to: the flesh or the spirit. How so? Because **the law of the Spirit of life in Christ Jesus** has made us free from **the law of sin and death**. It's a covenant of grace made in Christ Jesus for us. In it we are free from the law of sin and of death as we have a new nature in Christ.

> There is therefore now no condemnation to those who are in Christ Jesus, who do not walk according to the flesh, but according to the Spirit. For the law of the Spirit of life in Christ Jesus has made me **free** from the

law of sin and death (Romans 8:1-2 NKJV).

How are we free from the law of sin and death that we inherited from Adam? By receiving what Christ did for us. He paid the penalty for us according to the law. He came as human flesh on our behalf and allowed the condemnation of sin to be borne by Him, thereby releasing us from condemnation.

> For what the law could not do in that it was weak through the flesh, God *did* by sending His own Son in the likeness of sinful flesh, on account of sin: He condemned sin in the flesh, that the righteous requirement of the law might be fulfilled in us who do not walk according to the flesh but according to the Spirit (Romans 8:3-4 NKJV).

Is this exemption from condemnation available to all? No, this verse says that only those who are in Christ are exempt: "There is therefore now no condemnation to those **who are in Christ Jesus**" (Romans 8:1). The condition is to be in union with Him through belief in Him and to walk in the Spirit as flesh only leads to more sin and condemnation.

The Bible shows a distinct difference between those who walk in the Spirit and those who walk in the flesh. It's all a matter of the orientation of our mind:

> For those who live according to the flesh set their minds on the things of the flesh, but those *who live* according to the Spirit, the things of the Spirit. For to be carnally minded *is* death, but to be spiritually minded *is* life and peace. Because the carnal mind *is* enmity against God; for it is not subject to the law of God, nor

indeed can be. So then, those who are in the flesh cannot please God (Romans 8:5-8 NKJV).

The second thing to consider is who is the ultimate arbiter of our conscience? Does it rest with us? Look at what the Bible says, "For if our hearts condemn us, God is greater than our hearts, and knoweth all things. Behold, if our hearts condemn us not, then we have confidence toward God" (I John 3:20). So, even if our hearts condemn us in a matter, it is God who finally judges. He is superior in power and judgment over our heart and conscience.

UNPRODUCTIVE DISPUTES

Paul gave an illustration of the operation of our conscience in Romans 14. Here he discusses the dietary laws followed by those in Judaism compared with the practices of those coming into the Christian faith whether Jew or Gentile. Gentiles were not subject to the dietary laws of Judaism and were therefore free to eat any food they liked (except with blood). A Jew who had newly come into Christianity also had that freedom to eat whatever he chose; but it depended on his conscience whether he would keep within the dietary laws of Judaism or not. At the same time Paul argued such Jews should exercise restraint when eating in front of more traditionally-minded Jews for the sake of not "stumbling" their brother. "Therefore let us not judge one another anymore, but rather resolve this, not to put a stumbling block or a cause to fall in *our* brother's way" (Romans 14:13 NKJV).

In the last analysis, this principle concerns not only food but any area where there could be varying interpretations of right or wrong. While transgressing the laws of God is never in question, there are secondary matters, such as the observance of feasts and holy days, eating food offered to idols or drinking alcohol, that are open to interpretation. The guideline advocated by Paul is not to judge another because they do not share the same views, or refrain from doing things that offend a brother who thinks differently. Do not be distracted from kingdom business by causing unnecessary offense.

> Do not destroy the work of God for the sake of food. All things indeed *are* pure, but *it is* evil for the man who eats with offense. *It is* good neither to eat meat nor drink wine nor *do anything* by which your brother stumbles or is offended or is made weak (Romans 14:20-21 NKJV).

Whatever we do, therefore, let us do it with a clear conscience. If we are doubtful whether a thing is right or wrong, it is better to play safe and not do it. If, in spite of being in doubt, we go ahead and do it, we have sinned because we have not acted out of faith:

> Happy *is* he who does not condemn himself in what he approves. But he

who doubts is condemned if he eats,
because *he does* not *eat* from faith;
for whatever *is* not from faith is sin
(Romans 14:22-23 NKJV).

This is a wise teaching especially in gray areas, so, even if our conscience is clear, we should wait upon the Lord for His go-ahead signal before we act. "Therefore judge nothing before the appointed time; wait until the Lord comes. He will bring to light what is hidden in darkness and will expose the motives of the heart" (1 Corinthians 4:5 NIV).

"For if our heart condemns us, God is greater than our heart, and knows all things" (John 3:20) – so, in this case, wait. On the other hand, "if our heart does not condemn us, we have confidence toward God"(John 3:21). We then have the security that what we do is acceptable to Him.

In conclusion, those who are of good conscience towards God will be those who have set their hearts on the things of God and not on their sensual appetites. Their hearts have come to a place of rest in the security that whatsoever we have received of Him is good. As long as we do not allow ourselves to be controlled by our appetite towards worldly things or things that would harm our spiritual well-being, then we can say that in no way are our normal desires contrary to the will of God. It is the keeping of His commandments and being led by the Spirit that give us wholesome wishes and desires. And, if we set our minds to do those things that are pleasing to Him, we will not go contrary to His will or Word in all areas of life.

We read earlier how we can allow self-condemnation to dominate our conscience. Fear is the underlying motive. But what is the antidote? Read on to discover what it is.

Chapter Five

FEARLESS LOVE

Do you know that doors to the enemy are open because of lack of love? When God convicts our hearts where we have failed to display love, what do we do with the opportunity? What will it cost us? It will cost us our belief system concerning the boundaries we have set on giving love to others. But we will have to first receive God's kind of love that He commands us to give to others. We must then release the character and behaviors that correct this character flaw. Our security must always rest in our obedience to what God commands and not in the protective measures we set up in relation to others due to our lack of trust and security in them.

And God will reveal the faulty parts of our security system. We must become so secure in Him that it does not matter what others do to us. Our security should not be in a person's ability to do everything right or on the idea that they will never hurt or disappoint us. Even when these things appear, we must be solid as a rock in Jesus because He alone is our security and our fortress. Now that we are empowered with this truth, we can love others the way God intends us to.

Jesus said some radical things about love in Matthew 5:43-44:

> **Ye have heard** that it hath been said, Thou shalt love thy neighbor, and hate thine enemy. **But I say unto you**, love your enemies, bless them that curse you, **do good** to them that hate you, and **pray** for them which despitefully use you, and persecute you: That ye may be children of your Father which

is in heaven: for he maketh his sun to rise on the evil and on the good, and sendeth rain on the just and the unjust. For if ye love them which love you, what reward have ye? Do not even the publicans, the same? Be ye perfect, **even as** your Father which is in heaven is perfect.

What is our purpose in doing so? That we may be perfect like our Father. For, if we are truly His, we only bear His fruit both in character and behavior. This is the mark of His children. Compassion and consideration of others is a proper reflection of Him. As He is kind to the just and the unjust alike, let us show kindness and mercy to those who deserve it or don't. Lest we turn and forget what manner of person we are, let us remember that we were once enemies of God. How bountiful is His grace toward us to reconcile us to Himself so graciously! So with humility and meekness we are to portray the same to others, friends and foes alike.

Therefore let us aim to be perfect in heart and in deed, just as our Father in heaven is perfect. We are instructed to love our enemies. How often are we guilty and even prejudiced in adapting ourselves to people who are different from us? Oftentimes we look favorably only on those of whom we approve. Jesus wants us to have compassion toward all men regardless of their deeds. Why else would He give us a command to do so? In our ability or inability to do so we may reveal the true fabric of our hearts. The battle is lost or won here. If we think our enemies unworthy of this kind of love, it will be impossible to fulfill this command. When a man's ways please the Lord, He will make even His enemies to be at peace with him. This is not relative to the deeds of others but in spite of their deeds. Security is not required to love; it comes out of our obedience to God.

Jesus goes further to show the extent of our love. He instructs us to bless those who curse us, to pronounce words that call for divine favor upon those who curse us. To this, the Apostle Peter adds, "Don't repay evil for evil. Don't retaliate with insults when people insult you. Instead, pay them back with a blessing. That is what God has called you to do, and he will grant you his blessing" (I Peter 3:9 NLT). We are to walk in love not the world's way and not do to others what is done to us but what God has done for us. In our hearts should abide the law of kindness. Out of the abundance of the heart, only kindness will come forth from the mouth.

We are to do good to those that hate us, to be glad to show them kindness and be happy at the chance to do so. These are all opportunities for us to demonstrate the true nature and character of Christ. His dying words petitioned God to forgive those who crucified Him and to not lay a charge against them. We should find ourselves doing the same to those who have harmed us, our loved ones, our possessions – even our reputation.

Have you ever had that one person in your life who triggered every fear thing in your bucket list? I remember when I was a little girl, my mom either heard someone say something about me or it was reported to her: a man was expressing a desire toward me, a little girl of ten. My mom repeated the words to me. I had no idea what some of those words meant; nevertheless it sparked fear in me. It was that day fear entered my life. In that moment, all sense of security and protection was gone. I remember saying to myself that I would have to protect myself from now on, not even aware of what this truly meant. I somehow knew I did not have my sense of security anymore. I did not know who the enemy was or who I would be safe with.

This kind of fear followed me into my adult life and it impacted the way the way I raised my daughter. We lived a very sheltered and secluded life because of this. Once I had my daughter, then it became about keeping her safe. It was truly burdensome having to protect myself and now I needed to learn how to protect her. I had opened so many doors I would not have opened had it not been for the fear factor. What I had not created happened because I feared it. I either made the way or put myself in a position for it to happen.

It was not until I walked through each of my fears that I could see that I had worshiped the concept of security and safety more than I did God. I will not forget the day it all melted away. It was then I realized that I had longed for a state of security more than I did Jesus. This was the crux of the matter.

When we have the proper concept of His love for us, we begin to see that, when others do hurtful things to us, they are not doing it to us; they are really doing it to God. When Saul had his road to Damascus experience, the Lord asked him, "Saul, why persecutes thou Me?" Saul was persecuting His church, so what others do to the righteous they are in reality doing to Jesus. This is a great revelation to protect the heart from carrying human offenses. We must grab a hold of this as it will allow us to continue in love when we encounter suffering from the ones we love and from strangers.

This traumatic experience from my childhood had caused me to make security and safety my goal in life, looking for it in all the wrong places and people. But, at the completion of each phase of this bucket list and at the end of each hurt, I saw Jesus. In each moment He was bigger and more powerful than each of my fears. There was nothing else this person could do to me; neither did I fear him anymore because I realized Jesus was greater. This is how I came into this revelation of the security in Father God that Adam and Eve had lost. This is what caused them to come to the place of fear: they had lost this security in Father God to the accuser of the brethren. This is what caused them to fear judgment, and they hid.

This is where the enemy is lurking in the life of humanity. We constantly fear judgment because of our sinful nature and because of mistakes or mishaps in life, or some failure to keep an instruction by God. This causes us to feel a sense of unworthiness towards His goodness and blessings. Can you imagine what goes through our minds? We could be wondering, "Do you think He will forgive me? What do you think He will say to me? Do you think this is how I will die since I disobeyed Him? Do you think He will strike me dead?"

I can only imagine the questions that ran through Adam and Eve's minds and hearts. Their only recourse was to cover and hide themselves. But even in the midst of their new life outside the garden, He clothed them in proper garments suitable for the harshness of the environment. He assured them of redemption. Can you imagine what it was like to all of a sudden be overwhelmed by a new life apart from God? They had no concept of this kind of fear or the self-condemning conscience before.

SECURITY IN GOD'S LOVE

The heart must place its security in the assurance that God loves us and is true to His word just as Abram did when God told him, "I am your shield and your exceeding great reward." He took ownership of this truth from God to him. This sense of stability is so powerful that it precedes the rewards we receive from Him. He searches the heart and He yields to each one according to what is found there. The innermost part, which can only be seen and revealed by God, this part of our being must be girded with the truth of who He is. We must buy into His truth and not into the lies of Satan.

We have confidence in Him when we obey His command and we lose confidence when we do not. Our first parents lost their confidence in God because of their failure to be obedient to His instructions. This left a legacy of fear and shame upon all of humanity. This is the lure of Satan. If he can keep us operating in disobedience and displeasing God, then our confidence to come boldly before Him is broken, whereas, when we are operating in true obedience from a heart yielded to Him, we come boldly and ask. This same mentality is what opens the door to fear in our lives. The Bible states, immediately their eyes were opened, and when their conscience judged them, fear seized them. As believers I pray that we might be aware, be on the alert and guard ourselves against such self-condemning fear.

What does God want us to do when we have failed Him? The instructions are clear: own up and repent:

> If we claim we have no sin, we are only
> fooling ourselves and not living in the
> truth. But if we confess our sins to
> him, he is faithful and just to forgive

us our sins and to cleanse us from all wickedness. If we claim we have not sinned, we are calling God a liar and showing that his word has no place in our hearts (1 John 1:8-10 NLT).

If, on the other hand, Satan can keep us breaking the commands of God and displeasing Him without seeing the grace of forgiveness, he maintains his right of passage in our lives through the spirit of fear. When our confidence in God is sealed, there is perfect love and no fear in our hearts concerning the love of God toward us. But this cannot happen when that confidence is broken and we are afraid of God.

What is bringing about the fear in our lives? In my own personal experience, it happened when I was a little girl. But it goes back further. My mother was shaped in fear in her mother's womb and it was transferred to her. This can easily appear to have been the cause of my generational fear. Even so, since I was bent on finding the ultimate root, it had to be tracked down to the inception of this spirit and I realized it can be traced to what took place in the garden as the Holy Spirit began to reveal to me. It all started with disobedience and a desire to please ourselves above God.

How do we drive out the fear? Get rid of the disobedience and the self-love. Sin makes the conscience, and not God, the judge. The Bible reveals when the eye of their conscience was opened how they responded to their actions. The serpent told Eve her eyes would be opened to know good and evil. That eye was the eye of conscience, now open to judge them for what they had done. The conscience became the judge and jury. It caused them to testify against themselves. However, although they did admit to the deed, they never owned up to the sin in true repentance. They immediately condemned themselves without falling on their knees before the Father and seeing the power of His mercy and forgiveness.

Oh how we should want the eyes of our hearts to be opened to see Jesus! We must ask Him to open the eyes of our hearts so that we may see Him in all of His splendor and glory in power and in love. We would then see the full extent of our security in Him.

Diplomatic Immunity

Diplomatic immunity is a principle of international law by which certain foreign government officials are recognized as having legal immunity from the authority of another country. It allows diplomats safe passage and freedom to reside in a host country and affords them almost total protection from local lawsuits and prosecution.

Divine immunity is when we walk with purpose as ambassadors of Christ carrying out our functions in obedience to divine instruction and the total will of God. This immunity provides a protective covering for every believer in Christ, preserving us from sickness, disease, and all diabolical intrusion in the heart, mind, body, and spirit.

This immunity against the assignments of the kingdom of darkness is sealed with the Holy Spirit of promise until Christ returns for His own. Ephesians 1:13-14 tells us, "And grieve not the Holy Spirit of God whereby ye are **sealed unto the day of redemption**." "Sealed" has the idea of "fastening with a seal to prevent tampering" or "to close by a fastening against access, leakage, or passage." "To seal" in the Bible comes from the Greek word *sphragizō*, meaning "to stamp with a private mark for security from Satan." In other words, God has given us the Holy Spirit as our guarantee or down payment of redemption until the return of Christ, "who also has sealed us and given us the Spirit in our hearts as a guarantee" (2 Corinthians 1:22 NKJV).

What is included in Christ's redemption? Protection, Prevention, and Immunity. For what did Christ atone? Sin, sickness, pain, suffering, death, and demonic bondage. How did Christ redeem us? With His blood, His pain, His body and death to satisfy the debt required to make us free. This provision is identifiable in a believer: it is seen, made visible, made manifest or known. This allows the Holy Spirit to seal us until the day of redemption.

Is it enough to say we are healed and go on our way for redemption to take place? Consider the ten lepers who came to Jesus. They were all healed as they made their way to show themselves to the priest according to the law. But only one returned to Jesus to thank Him. Giving thanks is an act of worship. To that single worshiper, Jesus said, "Arise, go thy way: thy faith hath made thee **whole**" (Luke 17:19). Again, to the lame man Jesus healed at the pool at Bethesda, Jesus said, "Behold, thou art made **whole**: sin no more, lest a worse thing come unto thee" (John 5:14). You see, there is a distinction between "healed" and "made whole." The wholeness comes with the Holy Spirit. He is the sealing agent who marks you for Christ. Without that seal and protection, we are prone to returning to a life of sin.

This is why God sometimes does not remove our suffering, for suffering is a necessary condition for our being to be made whole. We can find purpose in suffering. We suffer to be broken to be made whole. We are emptied (of our pride and human ability) to be filled with the Holy Spirit. His indwelling Spirit abiding in us guards us and fortifies us. We can think of brokenness as a process; emptiness as the reason, and filled as the purpose. The final part, sanctification, is the cultivation of the fruit of the Spirit and its goal is **sonship** so that we mature from childhood and truly bear His image and likeness.

Having believed in Christ, we are sealed with the Holy Spirit of promise. He that has the Holy Spirit has the mark that he belongs to God.

> **... in whom also after** that you believed ye were **sealed** with the Holy

Spirit of promise, **Which** is the earnest of our inheritance **until** the redemption of the purchased possession unto the process of His glory (Ephesians 1:13-14).

We can be healed and delivered, but not filled but when we are not filled with the Holy Spirit, we are in a dangerous place because we have no security. Remember what Jesus said about being delivered from evil spirits:

> When the unclean spirit is gone out of
> a man, he walketh through dry places
> seeking rest, and findeth none. Then
> he saith, I will return into my house
> from whence I am out; and when he is
> cometh, he findeth it empty, swept and
> garnished. Then goeth he, and taketh
> with himself seven others spirits more
> wicked than himself, and they enter
> in and dwell there: and the last state of

than man is worse than the first. Even so shall it be also unto this wicked generation (Matthew 12:43-45).

We can be healed and delivered but not filled. But we must be filled to be made whole. The people who were made whole in the Bible were those who returned to worship Him, were filled with the Spirit and sealed unto the day of redemption when our Lord returns. That was their immunity against the wiles of Satan.

How does demonic intrusion come in? It creeps up from behind largely when we do not display the fruit of the Holy Spirit in our lives. Or we may refuse to cultivate the fruit required for each test, whether it be love, or patience or endurance. We need to continue in obedience to His word, to be found full of the fruit of the Spirit so that, when the enticement of sin is presented, we do not fall. Even if we should fall, the brunt of the whole law is not thrust upon us, leading to condemnation and judgment. No, we rise up and lay hold of our inheritance in Christ, repenting and being restored. Our frailty is always strengthened by walking in the Spirit.

Let us adopt His thoughts for our minds: "For who hath known the mind of the Lord, that he may instruct him? But we have the mind of Christ" (1 Corinthians 2:16).

Let us adopt His word for our mouth: "Let the words of our mouth and the meditation of our hearts be acceptable unto you" (Psalm 19:14).

Let us perform His deeds with our hands: "Whatsoever our hands find to do, we will do it heartily unto the Lord" (Colossians 34:23-24).

Let us find His path for our feet: "Your word is a lamp unto my feet and a light unto my path" (Psalm 119:105).

Note that all things need to be tested to prove their worth. Even the character of Jesus was tested in the wilderness before He was sent out with power for service (Luke 4:14).

With the right of refusal we are also tempted with an array of "good things" in religion. We are presented with a form of godliness, but in its true essence it is the denial of His power. Do not be one who denies His power by simply settling for a form or a past glory. When we find ourselves comfortable in this state, we build on the traditions or religion of man. Satan is the god of religion and the spirit behind traditionalism. We must oppose the enemy and not give ourselves over to his snares. We must resolve to refuse to accept defeat, or move on without receiving what God has promised in our intended need or desire. We need to stand on the promises we received by God. We must fortify ourselves to stand against the enemy and we must take the word at face value.

Jesus said that "man shall not live by bread alone, but by every word of God" (Luke 4:4). You must feed on the word of God daily as if your life depended on it. Not some today or none tomorrow, but be filled with His word all the time. It is the secure foundation of the believer to know His word so intimately that you know when to use it and how to execute it properly to bring forth power.

Jesus' parting words before He went to the Father were to take the gospel into all the world. What was the context? It was a context of unbelief – stony ground. Mark 16:13-14 says this:

> And they went and told it unto the residue: **neither believed they them**. Afterward he appeared unto the eleven as they sat at meat, and up-braided them with their unbelief and hardness of heart, because they be-lieved not them which had seen him after he was risen.

It was hard ground because of unbelief in Christ's resurrection. Nevertheless, the commissioning of the gospel takes place:

> And he said unto them, Go ye into all the world, and preach the gospel to every creature. He that believeth and is baptized shall be saved; but he that believeth not shall be damned.

> What is the evidence that the gospel has power? Signs and wonders.

> And these signs shall follow them that believe; In my name shall they cast out devils; they shall speak with new tongues; They shall take up serpents; and if they drink any deadly thing, it shall not hurt them; they shall lay hands on the sick, and they shall recover.

So then after the Lord had spoken unto them, he was received up into heaven, and sat on the right hand of God. And they went forth, and preached every where, the Lord working with them, and confirming the word with signs following. Amen (Mark 16:15-20).

The signs, wonders and miracles speak of the fullness of the Holy Spirit at work in people's lives, empowering them with supernatural ability. That is the mark of a true believer of Christ: filled with the Holy Spirit with boldness and faith to take the gospel to the ends of the earth with signs and wonders to prove God's endorsement.

If suffering is meant to test us, in the next chapter we will discuss our proper response to suffering and adversity.

SPIRITUAL COMBAT

Before we can react to adverse situations, we must first understand the nature of the Kingdom that we are now citizens in. When trouble shows up in our lives, we must start looking for the purposes of God in it. At such times, I have come to know and to trust it is the wind beneath my wings – time for me to soar into the will of God for His next assignment. Adversity is the wind of change. Start looking for the wind.

Is this not what happened when Jesus was brought before Pontius Pilate for interrogation? This was the signal of the next assignment given to Him by the Father. In the dialogue between Jesus and Pontius Pilate, Jesus reveals the Kingdom of which He is King. Pilate asks, "Art thou the king of the Jews?" (John 18:33) and Jesus' answer provides for us an overview of the kingdom of heaven and how it operates.

He says, "**My kingdom is not of this world:** if my kingdom were of this world, then would my servants fight, that I should not be delivered to the Jews: but now is my kingdom not from hence" (John 18:36).

Jesus takes this opportunity to assure Pilate that His Kingdom was not a threat to his man-made kingdom. He was not a king with any earthly interest at all. There are no earthly traits or components of it. His kingdom is not of this world: it is the kingdom of heaven. This is what the zealots failed to understand about Him when He used to hide Himself lest they try and make Him king.

This kingdom which He rules is a kingdom within an invisible realm: the heart. Its aim is to establish itself in the heart and the conscience of humanity, "for the kingdom of God is not meat and drink; but righteousness, and peace, and joy in the Holy Ghost" (Romans 14:17). This kingdom was once outwardly manifested in the earth until Adam gave its dominion over to Satan. What had been lost through Adam, Jesus came to reestablish among men. For now, this kingdom is in the inner life of men until the restoration of the earthly kingdom.

How does this kingdom operate? Everything about it and its operation is spiritual. Its battles are spiritual, its power is spiritual, its weapons are spiritual. Everything in it is contrary to the spirit of the world, which is why the weapons of our warfare cannot be used in the carnal domain. We cannot do warfare by human methods and hope to succeed. We have to use spiritual weapons enforced and empowered by God and Him alone. Moreover, this kingdom is not after any earthly government. Its true focus is the kingdom of darkness where Satan has his throne against the kingdom of righteousness. This is what the Kingdom of Heaven is set to oppose and to bring to destruction on earth as it is in heaven.

So, though we are in this world, we do not use its methods or depend on them. The foundation, the force, the power, the purpose, the security are all spiritual. The security we seek is met spiritually, not in earthly things or securities offered by the world. We use neither its wisdom nor its techniques. They must all be torn down and be replaced with a new mind and a new heart according to the will of God. New desires and appetites must be nurtured as led by the Spirit, and not by human dictates through the senses, emotions or feelings.

But this kingdom is being assailed on every side by the enemy. Therefore, we must not only defend it, we must **contend** for it. The Apostle Jude tells us, "Beloved, when I gave all diligence to write unto you of the common salvation, it was needful for me to … exhort you that ye should earnestly **contend** for the faith which was once delivered unto the saints" (Jude 1:3).

What does it mean to "contend"? "To contend" is "to strive for or vie for as in a contest or rivalry" or "to strive or contend against as in a struggle against an accuser." In the Christian context, it implies "to struggle upon appropriately with skill in opposing whatever is not of faith; to not exercise a right of refusal to anything to what was once delivered to the church."

How does this "right of refusal" operate? While I was in prayer one day, the Holy Spirit spoke to me and said, "When you change My word, you become a law unto yourself. This is exactly what happened to Eve when she added to the law of God and made her own law – she altered it by adding the word **touch** – "Ye shall not eat of it, **neither shall ye touch it**, lest ye die" was what she reported God had said (Genesis 3:3).

It is so crucial that we bind ourselves to the entire truth of His word, for every one of His words is truth. All else is fallacy and a lie, illuminated from the carnal mind and the wicked one. We are given over to what we give our belief system over to. When we give our belief system over to fear, fear will undoubtedly overtake us. Give it over to pride and lust, and they will dominate our thoughts. Whatever we give ourselves over to will lord over us.

Satan has a personal vendetta against God and he carries it out by making war on the saints to keep us from obtaining what we need from God. His demons make war constantly on the saints. How? Through bombarding the mind with false concepts about God in order to sow fear or unbelief just as he did with Eve to weaken her faith and trust in Him. He will succeed with us as well if we allow ourselves to fall prey to the wrong thought menu. The purpose of such ungodly thoughts that assail our mind is to keep us powerless, in poverty, in failure and to bring reproach upon God and His gospel. Satan is relentless in his efforts and will stop at nothing. His enemy is both God and man.

So how do we fight this battle? The Bible says:

> For though we walk in the flesh, we do not war after the flesh:(For the weapons of our warfare are not carnal, but mighty through God to the pulling down of strong holds …) (2 Corinthians 10:3-4)

For though we operate in a physical body in a material world in the natural affairs in life, we must remember we must not conduct this warfare from our carnal mind or use any of its strategies of war. Jesus put on the nature of the flesh, the appearance of it, the mind of the flesh, but He had to transcend His human nature each time He confronted a situation. He applied the word as a weapon to each problem He faced in the flesh.

For our weapons of our warfare are not carnal but mighty through God to the "pulling down of strongholds". How do we pull down strongholds? By "Casting down imaginations, and every high thing that exalteth itself against the knowledge of God, and bringing into captivity every thought to the obedience of Christ" (2 Corinthians 10:5). That's every thought – not just one or two of them – but subjecting every thought to the obedience of Christ. It's a constant resetting of the mind. A decision-making process is required to evaluate the motives and intents of each thought and to decide whether to accept it or reject it.

The weapons of our warfare are "mighty through God." They are empowered by Him and success in pulling them down is only through Him. So where do these strongholds lie? In the mind; in human reasoning and imaginations that will attempt to nullify or weaken the word of God and the gospel. As we entertain them, they fortify and secure themselves through the further intrusion of demonic powers. We cannot afford to mull over them. We must pull them down immediately to destroy them completely.

Satan's strategy against us is to use any vulnerability he perceives in our makeup – our ignorance of the topic, any prejudice, or our lust and propensity for a thing. He uses vain virtues such as ambition, fantasizing, carnal reasoning, or any thinking that is contrary to righteous thoughts. We must use the word of God to pull down Satan's institution of strongholds because the word is empowered and graced for us by God Himself.

All of Satan's efforts is to prevent man from belief and obedience to God. This is how he secures his hold on all hearts and lives that are not turned over to Jesus. Therefore, anything that attempts to exalt itself above God is what we are to classify as a "high thing" in our thought life. Pride is one of them; it is the hallmark of Lucifer. With pride comes independent thinking that leads us to any system, teaching or philosophy aimed at nullifying or denying the knowledge or truth of God. We are to take every one of these thoughts and imprison them as captives that must obey Christ.

The mind is the battleground and it is here that we are successful at winning the true battles in life. The first step is to identify the enemy who is against us. Lock in on him as the target. The next step is to identify which strategy he is using against you. God does not want us to be ignorant or powerless against the onslaughts of Satan. He has prepared us to win all spiritual combat against him. This is why we must use the word, rightly dividing it as we are instructed to. This is the strategy Christ has committed to empower the demolition of all of the enemy's weapons against us, for Jesus came that He might destroy the works of the devil.

CONTEND FOR THE FAITH

During a time of prayer, I inquired of the Lord regarding a season of trials I was going through. He responded, "Contend for the faith that was once delivered to the saints." This is required for your faith to get to where it needs to be. He said, "You can achieve what you have faith enough to believe for. Use the weapons I have given you; they are designed to strengthen your faith." This is what birthed the compilation of this book.

Every situation is an opportunity for us to contend for the faith that was once delivered to the church. How so, you may ask? You will need to contend against all of the fiery darts of the enemy. You must start by believing God in every situation in your personal life and endeavor. Strong, ongoing faith, is the required response to any attack of the enemy. Your faith will overcome the enemy the way God intends the believer to be built up as a conqueror.

We must not lose sight of our faith. We must keep it continually before us and stake everything on such faith. We must give faith a value system in our lives. Our faith is based on the original gospel of what was once delivered, the sound doctrine of truth. Do not be removed from it. Bind yourself to it and exercise a right of refusal when pressured to let it go. Never forsake it and never separate yourself from it. The enemy is always after the word that has been planted. We must understand this and hold on to it until we see the promised harvest. Recognizing times and seasons in life will help you to approach it with understanding and patience.

Belief is a choice we make: to believe is to exercise the God-given power of choice. Yes, we are finite and limited in our capacity, but even in this limited ability, we are at liberty to choose wisely. He did not make us to be enslaved. We can contend because God gave us the faith necessary to believe the truth of who He is, His word and His provision for all our needs and circumstances. When we exercise faith properly, we become secure in God and not in the world around us. This is where the greatest battle will be lost or won. Belief is a state or habit of mind in which trust or confidence is placed in both the person and the thing we give our allegiance to.

Doubt made its entrance when the serpent caused Eve to rethink what God had said. It is part of our sin-inherited nature. In John 20 we also read about doubting Thomas. Here is an example of an "unbelieving" believer who refused to believe unless he had a direct personal encounter with Christ. As Thomas did not see the risen Christ, he refused to believe He had risen based on the accounts of the other disciples. No, he wanted to see and feel Jesus' wounds firsthand.

Compare the skepticism of Thomas with the nobleman whose son was critically ill and he requested Jesus to come and heal him.

> Then said Jesus unto him, Except ye
> see signs and wonders, ye will not be-
> lieve. The nobleman saith unto him,
> Sir, come down ere my child die.
> Jesus saith unto him, Go thy way;

thy son liveth. And the man **believed the word** that Jesus had spoken unto him, and he went his way. And as he was now going down, his servants met him, and told him, saying, Thy son liveth. Then inquired he of them the hour when he began to amend. And they said unto him, Yesterday at the seventh hour the fever left him. So the father knew that it was at the same hour, in the which Jesus said unto him, Thy son liveth: and himself believed, and his whole house (John 4:48-53).

The man believed Jesus at His word. Very often we are to believe without signs or anything visible. Those who can summon up their faith to believe are blessed. Jesus told Thomas, "You believe because you see. However, blessed are they who believe who have not seen!" In other words, "Your belief required proof of My resurrection but blessed are those who can and will come to this resolve without proof based solely on the exercise of their faith."

Thomas refused to believe without the standard of his proof being met, which revealed the power of his use of choice. He chose how he would allow himself to come to the state of believing in the resurrection of Jesus.

What is our required standard of proof to believe? What is our measure of faith?

> For I say, through the grace given unto me, to every man that is among you, not to think *of himself* more highly than he ought to think; but to think soberly, according as God hath dealt to every man the measure of faith (Romans 12:3).

"To measure" is "to allot or apportion in measured amounts; to estimate or assess the extent, quality, value or effect of something." In Greek, the word *metron* (Strongs 3358 "standard, measure") is the controlling basis by which something is determined as acceptable or unacceptable. God gives every man the power to believe, so man must exercise his power of choice. Note that doubting Thomas took the stance he would not believe until he saw proof according to the standard he had set for himself.

He who began a good work in us is faithful to the completion of the work He began. So where do you place your security? How is it defined in relation to God and His dealings with us? You must believe in His love for you and solidify it in your life. Your loins or your belief system must be properly girded with this truth. Everything hinges on this fundamental truth.

You will need this to guard against self-judgment and condemnation, fault- finding and critical-thoughts. "O LORD, you have examined my heart and know everything about me" (Psalm 139:1

NLT). I love how the song *Indescribable* puts it: "You see the depths of my heart and you love me the same." The investigation must begin here. Delve into and find out what you truly believe about God and His love for you. Belief in God is your support. The fundamentals of the whole armor of God will need to be revisited here. This is your first order of business if your true quest is the faith that was once delivered to the church. If not, you will be tossed and driven by a tempest.

The serpent was able to deceive Eve because she allowed him to tamper with her belief system. The entrance of doubt made its debut here on earth. It's an age-old technique, no different now. This is one of the greatest tactics of the enemy against us. However, it can only work in the hearts of men who choose not to solidify the love of God in their hearts. To deal with it effectively, we must first deal with doubt.

BROKEN TRUST LEADS
TO TRUE SECURITY

The development of security in God comes only when our trust has been broken, mishandled, damaged or violated. It is here that the believer will see the faulty parts of his belief system and discover it is not supported in God. We then come to appreciate how our trials and suffering have shown up as broken trust. God allows us to pluck up our tarnished belief system and allow Him to plant in us a proper system secured in Him. It is the irritation in the oyster that brings out beauty: the pearl. The right irritation in us will produce the pearl. Our tests and trials are there to produce the irritation that produces pearls. This is in accordance with God's purpose and will to bring forth a proper system secured in Him.

This knowledge will enable us to love properly – with abandonment – to love not for the sake of security or out of duty but to love in spite of the actions of others, regardless of the good or bad they do. That's the way we are commanded to in I John 4:7-21. Look at these verses:

> 7 Beloved, let us love one another: for love is of God; and every one that loveth is born **of God, and knoweth God.** 8 He that loveth not knoweth not God; for God is love. 9 In this was manifested the love of God toward us, because that God sent his only begotten Son into the world, that we might live through him. 10 Herein is love, not that we loved God, but that he loved us, and sent his Son to be the propitiation for our sins. 11 Beloved, if God so loved us, we ought also to love one another ... 16 ... God is love; and he that dwelleth in love dwelleth in God, and God in him.

[18] There is no fear in love; but perfect love casteth out fear: because fear hath torment. He that feareth is not made perfect in love. [19] We love him, because he first loved us. [20] If a man say, I love God, and hateth his brother, he is a liar: for he that loveth not his brother whom he hath seen, how can he love God whom he hath not seen? [21] And this commandment have we from him, That he who loveth God love his brother also.

As we mature in our faith, we must exemplify the same grace given to us by God to others without fear of harm. Even with those who may set themselves as enemies against us, we are instructed to love. This is the foundation to walking in the unconditional love required to operate in true obedience to His word.

My Testimony

On June 04, 2012, I left work and decided to go by the emergency room on my way home. I was pregnant. Something didn't feel right and I could literally see death on me; it was an extremely dark season of my life. I told the front desk person in the emergency room that I felt like I needed to be checked out. She looked at me and said, "Ma'am there is something more" and immediately called the birth and delivery unit.

After a number of tests, I was informed that my body was producing too much of something and that my vital organs were shutting down. For this reason the baby would have to be delivered by cesarean section the next day. By 2:30 p.m. the next day I was in surgery. When they delivered her, the doctor said, "Oh my, the umbilical cord was wrapped around her neck three times!" The tears began to fall. I knew in that moment that God allowed my body to go into distress because my baby was in distress.

We may not always understand His plan but we must learn to trust Him in spite of our lack of understanding.

After the surgery, I was told that the scar would remain and, since the nerves were severed it was not likely that I would regain sensation in that area. A week later I developed what is called a hematoma, which turned out to be a large blood clot in the area that was bonded back together from the cesarean. The clot forced its way out and the glue was literally ripped apart from the incision. They had to go back in and remove the hematoma which left a wound in the area, which had to be cleaned many times a week, ten weeks in all. I accepted all this as a part of the aftermath of a cesarean in addition to knowing that it saved both of our lives.

In August 2023, I was praying and asking God for optimal health. In September 2023, I was doing abs exercises in the gym and I felt a tear in my abdomen area. Well, the trainer checked the area and said it happened because the area had not been used. (I have maintained an exercise regimen on and off during the years so I knew this was not the case. This had never happened during other times of working out or during a time of stretching.) So I said, "No, you don't understand – there has been no feeling in this area for over eleven years. Now I can feel every move, every exercise!" Once I made it home I began to investigate the area and I had complete feeling in that area. I just kept touching it and there was complete feeling. Praise God!

I was reminded about the recent prayer and I remember thinking He could not give this to me before because I had accepted the report from the doctor. I had learned to live in the discomfort of not having sensations and I did not bother to inquire of Him concerning it. To be honest, I had forgotten about it. It's like He was saying to me, "I did not forget, but I waited until you gave Me the **right of passage** to take care of this for you." The prayer of faith opened the door for Him to do the best for me in the same way He desires the best for all of us. He does not want us to go without any of the benefits made available to us by His Son.

However, our faith is required to see the performance of His word. Will you contend and choose to remain steadfast until you see the full manifestation of His every promise fulfilled in your life? Our God is able, and He will do exactly what He has said He will do. He will fulfill every promise that He made in His word and those He has made to you individually. To see them, you must not give up on Him; you must remain steadfast and leave the logistics of how and when up to Him. His promise is His promise and He will fulfill every promise in its season.

Strength and Blessings!

Notes

Merriam-Webster: America's Most Trusted Dictionary

Wikipedia

Dakes Annotated Reference Bible The Old and New Testament, with notes, Concordance and Index @ Copyright holders Melanie Dake, Edward Finnis Dake, Monique Germaine, Kimberly Dake Kennedy, Kathryn Dake Iglinksi and Dake Ministries Lawrenceville, Georgia KJV Edition @ Copyright 2014 Fifth Printing – December 2019

Matthew Henry's Commentary On The Whole Bible New modern addition Complete and Unabridged in Six Volumes Copyright @ 1991 by Hendrickson Publishers, Inc. Seventh Printing – January 2003

Holman Illustrated Bible Dictionary, Revised and Expanded @ 2015 by B&H Publishing Group Nashville, Tennessee

https://biblehub.com/greek/4102.htm

https://bibleptoject.com/articles/gods-gives-job-tour-wise-world/#:-text=God%20asks%20job20call%of,"%20(38%3A19

Made in the USA
Monee, IL
07 July 2026